The Best You

MAKING THINGS Right

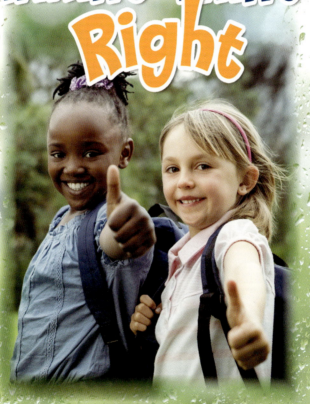

Dona Herweck Rice

Consultants

Diana Herweck, Psy.D.

Publishing Credits

Rachelle Cracchiolo, M.S.Ed., *Publisher*
Conni Medina, M.A.Ed., *Managing Editor*
Nika Fabienke, Ed.D., *Series Developer*
June Kikuchi, *Content Director*
Michelle Jovin, M.A., *Assistant Editor*
Lee Aucoin, *Senior Graphic Designer*

TIME For Kids and the TIME For Kids logo are registered trademarks of TIME Inc. Used under license.

Image Credits: p.11 Camille Tokerud Photography Inc./Getty Images; p.12 Alys Tomlinson/Getty Images; all other images from iStock and/or Shutterstock.

All companies and products mentioned in this book are registered trademarks of their respective owners or developers and are used in this book strictly for editorial purposes; no commercial claim to their use is made by the author or the publisher.

Teacher Created Materials

5301 Oceanus Drive
Huntington Beach, CA 92649-1030
http://www.tcmpub.com

ISBN 978-1-4258-4964-1

© 2018 Teacher Created Materials, Inc.

Table of Contents

Choices 4

Hurt Feelings 10

I Am Sorry 14

How to Make Amends 18

Be the Best You 26

Glossary 28

Choices

What clothes will I wear? What will I eat? Where will I go? What will I do?

Each day, we have many **choices** to make. Some choices are easy, such as deciding what to wear. Other choices are much harder. Those choices show what kind of people we want to be, especially in our relationships with others.

Relationships

A relationship is the way that two or more people or things get along. Family members have important relationships. Friends have important relationships, too.

We can choose to get along with other people. To do that, we must treat them with kindness. We use friendly words and actions. We should treat ourselves this way, too!

The important thing to remember is that how we act is *always* a choice. Each of us is in **control** of what we think, say, and do.

Relationships are not just between people.

But no one is perfect. We do not always make the right choices. This is especially true when we feel hurt, angry, or sad. It may seem hard to act with kindness then. We may even forget we have choices. We may just act before thinking.

Hurt Feelings

A big part of being human is having feelings. Sometimes, we feel joy. But our feelings can also be hurt. Sometimes, our choices hurt other people's feelings. We might even do it when we do not mean to. But there is good news! Hurt feelings can be healed.

The first step toward feeling better is to talk about your feelings.

One way we can be a good person is to choose to make **amends** after we hurt someone. Amends help heal hurt feelings.

When someone shows they are sorry, we should choose to **forgive** them. It helps us feel all right again.

What If?

What if someone who hurt you does not make amends? Can you be happy again? Yes, of course. Let yourself feel sad or angry about it. Then, let it go if you can. Giving it more attention keeps the hurt alive.

Making amends keeps relationships strong.

I Am Sorry

The first step to forgiveness is three little words. They are: "I am sorry." These words mean that the speaker knows he or she has hurt someone else. It means the person accepts that harm was done.

Some people have a hard time saying these words. It takes a strong person to say them.

I Forgive You

What should you say when someone says, "I am sorry"? The best response is, "I forgive you." It means that you accept their **apology**. You make a choice to heal and move on.

Being the Bigger Person

"I am sorry" can be hard to say when both sides feel hurt. But someone has to start. It is normal to want the other person to speak first. But if you do not take the first step, it may not happen. It takes **courage** to speak first. You can do it!

Bigger Person?

Being the bigger person does not have anything to do with size. It means being a person who shows courage. The bigger person does the right thing first—even when it is hard to do.

If you hurt someone's feelings, start by saying, "I am sorry."

How to Make Amends

Saying "I am sorry" is a key step. Saying "I forgive you" is important, too. But the hardest part of making things right comes from making amends.

To make amends is to do something to fix a mistake. Words alone do not make things right. Actions must make things right, too.

Types of Offense

The type of amends depends on the **offense**. A small offense needs a small amends. A big offense needs a big one.

What if Alek spills milk on Kate's homework? It is an accident. Alek says, "I am sorry." Then, he cleans up the milk. He also helps to fix her homework. In these ways, Alek makes amends for a small offense.

What if June makes Rachel mad, so Rachel throws a ball at June? That is a big offense. First, Rachel should say, "I am sorry." She can offer comfort to June as well. Then, she should promise never to do such a thing again. She must prove to June that she can be trusted. It will take time to earn back June's trust.

Comfort

To give comfort to another person is to care for them. Comfort might come in the form of a warm smile. It might be a hug. It might even be a warm cup of cocoa and a cozy blanket!

If you hurt someone, make amends by comforting them.

Taking Responsibility

The key to making amends is taking responsibility. You must show that you know that you hurt someone. The first step is to try to make things right again. If you cannot, you can at least make things better.

It is not always easy to make amends. But it is the right thing to do.

Dear Joe,

Sorry I threw your shoes in the tree.

-Bret

This boy helps his friend get his shoes out of a tree.

Be the Best You

It is up to each of us to be the best person we can be. We can be our best by saying, "I am sorry," if we hurt other people. We can also say, "I forgive you." But the most important thing is to make amends. Amends make things right and go a long way toward healing hurt feelings.

By doing these things, you make a choice to be the best *you* that you can be!

Be Kind

Sometimes, your friends and family hurt your feelings. But most of the time, they do not mean to. Do not be too quick to judge another person. A little kindness goes a long way!

Glossary

amends—things done to fix a mistake

apology—something you say or write that tells someone you are sorry

choices—decisions made between two or more things

control—power over something or someone

courage—the ability to do something that you know will be hard

forgive—to stop blaming or feeling anger toward someone

offense—something that causes someone pain or anger